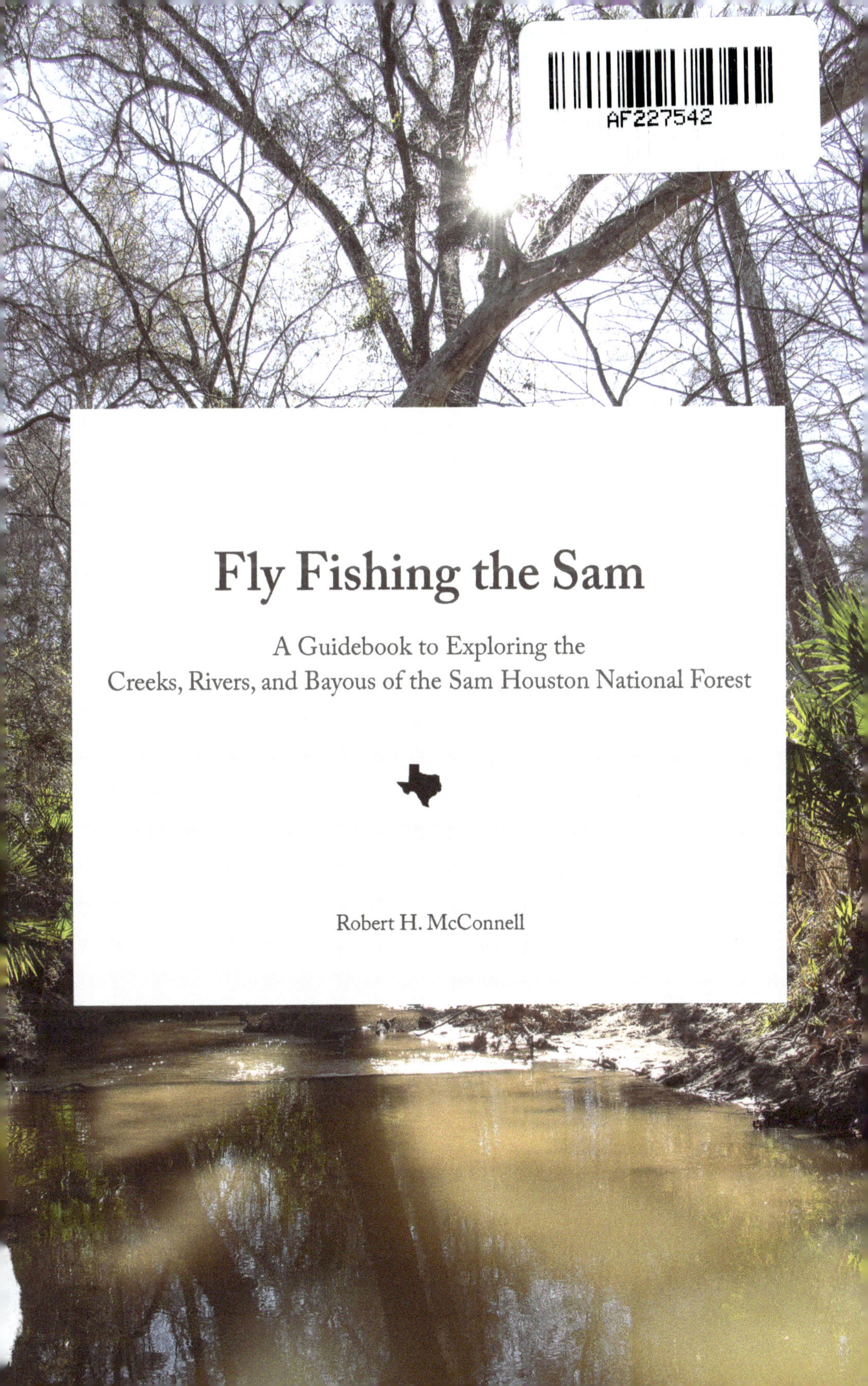

Fly Fishing the Sam

A Guidebook to Exploring the
Creeks, Rivers, and Bayous of the Sam Houston National Forest

Robert H. McConnell

Printed in the U.S.A.

Words: Robert H. McConnell

Cover design and interior book design: Robert H. McConnell

Editing: Sarah Townsend

Maps and figures: Robert H. McConnell (Maps were created with the help of onXmaps (www.onxmaps.com)

Photographs: Robert H. McConnell (except where stated otherwise)

Sport fish vector art: Jongseok Oh - follow him on social media @famza_art

Any web addresses mentioned in this book are subject to change since publication. The views and theories expressed in this book are solely those of the author. They do not necessarily reflect the views of any cited author, business, or person mentioned within.

Attention!

As a user of this book, you assume all risk associated with the activities described within. Like many outdoor activities, exploring and fishing the wilderness areas of the Sam Houston National Forest can potentially place you in dangerous situations. The author and publisher of this book provide no guarantee of the accuracy of the information in these pages and assume no responsibility for any injuries that may occur while exploring the waterways of the Sam. It is up to you, the reader, to always be prepared and vigilant of your surroundings.

A portion of the profits from the sale of this guidebook will be donated to various outdoor recreational causes. This includes, but is not limited to, the conservation of American wildlife and water resources, outdoor education, and further promotion of the American heritage of hunting, trapping, and fishing.

ISBN: 978-1-7344342-0-0 (pb)

ISBN: 978-1-7344342-1-7 (hc)

ISBN: 978-1-7344342-2-4 (e)

Library of Congress Control Number: 2020901796

For all my fishing buddies,
past, present, and future

Table of Contents

Acknowledgments 6

Preface 7

Introduction 9

What is the Sam Houston National Forest? 10

Stewardship 12

Laws related to camping in the Sam 13

Safety considerations for fishing the Sam 13

Equipment 16

Techniques for small-stream fishing 17

Fish handling 20

How to use this book 21

The Water 25

Western Sam Houston National Forest 28

Northern Sam Houston National Forest 38

Eastern Sam Houston National Forest 44

The Fish 59

Panfishes (*Lepomis*) 61

Black Basses (*Micropterus*) 69

Conclusion 75

Fly shops in the greater Houston area 76

Craft breweries between Houston and the Sam 77

Worthy Causes 78

Endnotes 79

Index of Waterways 82

Species List 83

Acknowledgments

A huge thank you to Kevin Conway, Associate Professor and Curator of Fishes at Texas A&M University. Professor Conway was instrumental in helping me with the identification of fish species and making sure that this simple angler didn't write anything too scientifically inept. Professor Conway's insights into ichthyology and the use of scientific citations was invaluable. I can't thank you enough, Professor!

Another huge thank you to Aaron Reed, author of *Fly Fishing Austin & Central Texas,* for the kind words of encouragement. Aaron graciously and happily betaread *Fly Fishing the Sam* and provided valuable feedback that undoubtedly improved the quality of the book. Thank you so much for your help, Aaron!

Preface

Five years ago, my wife and I moved from Western Pennsylvania to Houston, Texas. We left behind a rural lifestyle where the subjects of many dinner conversations involved fishing and hunting. It was a drastic change to move from the northern boonies down to the Gulf Coast and the fourth largest city in the country.

When we first made the move, I found it difficult to pursue the outdoor hobbies I loved so dearly. Since then, I have learned that I can still pursue my passion for the outdoors; I just have to spend a little more time in the car. By driving north, away from the city, I have found great joy in fly fishing the waters of the Sam Houston National Forest. This national forest is a peaceful place to escape the fast-paced urban lifestyle.

In the past, I have jotted down notes and journal entries about fly fishing in the Sam Houston National Forest, and it is these writings that I have compiled to produce this simple guidebook. This guide is designed for someone who enjoys striking out on their own, discovering hidden creeks, and angling for new fish species. The GPS waypoints found in this guide are merely a starting point for a fly fishing journey. Purposefully, I have only disclosed the waypoints for recommended places to park. I did my best to give written directions from the parking areas to the specific waterways, but I was intentionally vague to avoid divulging the exact locations of honey holes. My hope is that readers will discover the beauty and great angling in these watercourses on their own.

The wilderness streams, creeks, and bayous of this national forest deserve admiration, attention, and respect. I hope this little guide can be used as a tool to inspire Houstonians or new Houston transplants with a desire to discover unique lotic ecosystems. I hope it will help someone escape the concrete jungle and find peace while fishing the waters of a woodland stream in the Sam Houston National Forest.

Blue dasher dragonfly on West Sandy Creek

Introduction

What is the Sam Houston National Forest?

Sam Houston National Forest, or the Sam, is located about sixty miles north of downtown Houston, Texas. It comprises 161,500 acres of heavily forested terrain. It spans three counties: San Jacinto, Montgomery, and Walker. Established in 1933, the Sam is currently managed by the United States Forest Service. These lands are open to the public and operate under a multiuse philosophy. Thus, logging, oil production, cattle grazing, hunting, hiking, and other outdoor activities all take place within the boundaries of this national forest.[1] The Sam also includes the waters of Lake Conroe, a 20,000-acre lake, known by most Houstonians for its pleasure boating and fishing. A quick internet search reveals many resources dedicated to the fishing scene on Lake Conroe. This brief guide will not be another description of this well-known lake. My aim in writing this work is to draw attention to the little-known fisheries that exist in the wild and beautiful creeks, streams, and bayous that flow under a dense canopy of pines and hardwoods within the Sam Houston National Forest.

Regional map showing the location of the Sam Houston National Forest in relation to the city of Houston.

Why fish the Sam?

Writing about small waterways may seem like an odd subject to some readers. Why focus on small creeks when big bass can be caught in the local lakes from the bow of a powerboat? This is a legitimate question, and in no way am I knocking the fantastic fishing experiences that can be found on lakes throughout East Texas. Admittedly, hooking into an eight-pound bass on a fly rod is something that I have experienced too few times. However, to many fly anglers, a wilderness fly fishing experience is often just as important as catching a lunker. The adventure and tranquility that's felt away from the popular lakes and the whirr of boat motors can yield some of the greatest fishing experiences an angler can have. By fishing small streams, the angler is connected to the water in a unique way. It's a metamorphosis from a casual observer of nature into a participant.

By hiking in and fishing small waterways, the angler will observe the nuances of nature that are often overlooked when fishing from a powerboat. For instance, as you walk along a stream you'll look down at the sandy bank under your feet. There you'll notice tracks from raccoons and river otters. These master anglers trotted along the very same bank the night before. As you continue to hike and fish, each meander of the stream will bring a longing to know what lies beyond the next. By traversing muddy terrain, leaping fallen logs, and ducking through patches of cane, you'll slowly begin to uncover the mysteries of the stream. You'll feel like part of the ecosystem as you wade into the swirling water, the cool liquid gently pulling at your legs. You'll slip a hook from the mouth of a bass you just caught from under a sunken log as the dappled light dances on the flowing current and the hum of cicadas fills the air. After admiring your catch, you'll hold the bass under its belly and lower it into the water. There will be a brief pause before the fish realizes it's free. Whoosh! It's gone, back under the logjam from which you caught it.

By looking at a watershed map of the Sam Houston National Forest, you'll notice there are many streams not recognized in this book. Most of these streams were omitted because they lack sufficient waterflow to sustain a population of fish year-round. In order for a watercourse to be included in these pages, a few criteria had to be met:

1. The body of water is located within the boundaries of the Sam Houston National Forest and is accessible by the general public.
2. The watercourse can be accessed by foot.
3. The body of water contains fish that will readily take a fly (e.g., panfish and bass).
4. The body of water can be fished with a fly rod. The area surrounding the waterway must be generally free of obstructions, at least enough to perform a roll cast.

I'm not so bold as to make the claim that this book has addressed all the fishable waters within the national forest. It has not. There are many more bodies of water that can be explored and fished. My hope in writing this book is merely to whet the appetites of small-stream anglers in the Houston area. There are a plethora of small ponds and creeks left to explore within the Sam. Grab your rod and get going!

Stewardship

Houstonians are fortunate to have such a great fishery so close to home. This comes with the responsibility of being good stewards of our natural world. Be sure to always pack out the trash that you packed in. Keeping the waterways clean should be a top priority for all anglers.

For human waste, it is important to always dig a cathole. Make sure to dig the hole about seventy paces away from the creek, trails, and/or camp.[2] Select a site that is concealed, and dig the cathole six to eight inches deep. Be sure to place the used toilet paper in the cathole, and make sure to cover the hole back up when finished.

I don't always subscribe to the catch and release philosophy. Fresh fish on occasion can make for a wonderful dinner. Please be sure to harvest local fish in a responsible manner and never waste this natural resource. Always abide by Texas Parks and Wildlife regulations and laws.[3] Be sure to check size requirements and daily bag limits before harvesting fish.

We are incredibly blessed to live in a country that still holds wildlife and nature in high regard. We must always respect the natural world and do our best to keep our waterways flowing clean and teaming with fish. Always remember to be a good steward of nature.

Laws related to camping in the Sam

Sam Houston National Forest is different than most national forest lands because its entire acreage is designated as a Wildlife Management Area (WMA) by the Texas Parks and Wildlife Department. This designation makes the laws stricter when compared to many other national forest lands. During the hunting season, usually September 1 to February 1, camping is only permitted at designated campsites. These designated sites include developed recreation areas and hunter camps. Outside of hunting season (after February 1 and before the next hunting season), primitive camping is allowed throughout the forest, except where it's specifically prohibited. It is entirely possible to enjoy a wilderness fishing and camping trip within the Sam Houston National Forest. Just be sure to camp during the times of the year when it is legal. More information about camping can be found on the USDA Forest Service website.[4]

Safety considerations for fishing the Sam

The forests of East Texas are a unique place to fly fish. The climate, flora, and fauna make for an unforgettable angling experience. Even though the Sam Houston National Forest lies one hour north of Houston, it should still be considered genuine wilderness and full of wild things. A cell phone signal is nonexistent along many of the streams outlined in this work. The following are a few safety items that should be considered before hiking in and hitting the water.

Weather and climate

In the summer, East Texas is hot and humid. July and August are the hottest months, with temperatures hovering around the mid-90s to 100s during the day and an average humidity of 71 percent. Conversely, December and January usually have fluctuating temperatures ranging from the mid-40s to the mid-60s, while the humidity remains about the same. The temperature in the spring and fall is very pleasant.[5]

Because of the high temperatures during the summer months, it is imperative that you bring water and take frequent breaks. Your body can easily overheat due to the ambient temperature and physical exertion of hiking along the creeks.

Navigation

To folks born and raised along the Gulf Coast and East Texas, this topic will seem trivial. But to a person like me, from the Appalachian foothills—who is used to navigating by topographic landmarks—this is a significant subject to address. In areas of the country with more topography, it is easy to orient yourself by using far-off mountaintops as navigational markers. But directing yourself through the flat landscape and dense thickets of the Piney Woods can be challenging. The dense undergrowth in the summer months prevents you from seeing any distinct features of the terrain. Off-trail hiking and bushwhacking lead to remote, unpressured fishing holes, but if you choose to leave the trail, pay close attention to your direction of travel. It's hard to get your bearings when everything around you looks like the same thicket you just busted through. It's best to carry some kind of tool to help with navigation, whether it's a compass and map, handheld GPS, or the GPS on your phone.

Critters

Ticks – Sam Houston National Forest harbors a variety of ticks. The lone star tick, American dog tick, and brown dog tick are the most common. There are some occurrences of the dreaded deer tick, the carrier of Lyme disease, but they are uncommon.[6] Most ticks can transmit a multitude of diseases, and it's best to avoid being bitten by one. To prevent this from happening, use bug spray and tuck your shirttail into your pants. By doing this, you'll reduce your chances of having your blood sucked by one of these tiny parasites.

Snakes - The South is home to many different species of snakes, some of which can cause a hasty trip to the ER. The venomous serpents that live in Texas include copperheads, cottonmouths (water moccasins), rattlesnakes, and coral snakes. Most snakes in the state are nonvenomous, but unless you can make the distinction, it's best to leave all snakes alone. The two venomous snakes I see frequently are the cottonmouth and copperhead. Cottonmouths are semiaquatic. Their diet consists of fish and other aquatic creatures. This is the most common venomous snake seen by anglers while fishing the Sam. Be careful when stomping around logjams by the water, as this is great habitat for cottonmouths.

Copperhead found along Winters Bayou

Cottonmouth showing off its namesake

Hunting season

Only 4.2 percent of the landmass of Texas is open to the general public for hunting.[7] This makes areas like the Sam Houston National Forest a popular destination for hunters looking to fill the freezer with venison or wild pork. The Sam's close proximity to Houston ensures a fairly constant stream of hunters moving in and out of the national forest, especially during rifle season, which is most of November and December. Texas law states that on public land, rifle hunters are required to wear 400 square inches of fluorescent orange, the equivalent of a vest and hat. If you plan on fishing in the Sam during deer season, I recommend that you also wear fluorescent orange. Doing so will reduce your chances of being involved in a hunting accident.

Equipment

Most fly rodders know what gear is essential for hitting the stream, so I won't delve too deeply into the subject of gear and equipment. I will outline basic pieces of kit that I have found helpful and unique for fishing streams in the Sam. I usually abide by the KISS principle: keep it simple, stupid. Remember you'll be carrying this gear on your back all day. Do yourself a favor and only bring what you're going to use.

Throughout most of the year, East Texas is warm enough for wet wading. However, the water can be chilly during the winter months. Wading pants that can be packed in a backpack are ideal for when the water is cold. I would advise against wearing the specialized wading boots designed for fly fishing. These boots are not practical for the muddy creek banks of East Texas. You're better off wearing old hiking boots that cover your ankles. If you have the coin, a specialized water shoe like Astral's Rassler or Brewer is an excellent choice. DO NOT wear sandals while wet wading in East Texas. If you do, your feet will endure a severe beating. Most of the time in the summer, I wear nylon snake gaiters over my hiking boots and pants. I do this not because of the snakes (although it does give me peace of mind), but because it minimizes the amount of debris that will make its way into my shoes.

The rods I use most often vary between a 7.5-foot 3-weight and an 8.5-foot 5-weight. If I'm angling for panfish and flinging small flies (hook sizes 10 and smaller), I'll use the 3-weight. If I'm casting bigger flies for bass (hook sizes 8 to 4), I'll use the 5-weight. I've found the 5-weight to be the most versatile and dependable rod for fishing the majority of creeks in the Sam.

Short leaders work best on the streams of the Sam. The fish aren't leader shy, and they can't see the leader in the cloudy water. I often tie 6- to 7.5-foot leaders for the smaller streams like Big Creek and West Sandy Creek, while 7.5- to 9-foot leaders work well on the larger creeks. I terminate the leader with tippet ranging in size from 2X (.009 inches) up to .014 inches.

For flies, you don't need anything fancy. Panfish and bass aren't too picky, and they eat just about anything on topwater and subsurface. I like fishing gurglers on topwater and wooly buggers, streamers, or soft hackle flies for subsurface. A size 8 hook is good for catching both bass and panfish. A specific fly I have used with fantastic results is Danny Scarborough's Brasshawk. Originally, this was tied as a carp fly, but it works well on just about any species of fish in the waters of the Sam.[8]

When there isn't much daylight penetrating into the water, either due to cloud cover or silt in the water, it's best to angle with dark-colored flies. Conversely, on bright and clear days, angle with light-colored flies. Terry and Roxanne Wilson explain in their book *The Bluegill Diaries: A Fly Fishing Chronicle*, "Light colors such as white, yellow and tan are effective under bright conditions because they reflect the most light and can be seen from longer distances by the fish. If on the other hand, the sun is near the horizon or shielded by clouds and the water is stained, a dark pattern will present the strongest silhouette as viewed by the bluegills."[9]

Techniques for small-stream fishing

Over the years of fishing small streams, I have found that certain techniques work better than others. Forget about casting a beautiful double haul. This will cause your fly to be hung in the trees more often than not. Keep your casts simple and tight. By merely mending or flipping the fly line, you can present a well-placed fly that will entice a fish to strike. The following is a list of casts in order of how often I use them while fishing small streams:

1. Roll cast
2. Bow-and-arrow cast
3. Backhand cast
4. Steeple cast

I won't go into detail on what these casts look like, but if you'd like more information on them, A. D. Livingston talks about these techniques in his book *Bass on the Fly*.[10]

Once the cast is made and the fly is in the water, I prefer to strip line with my free hand, keeping the line straight with the rod tip down. Many bass fly fishermen harp on keeping your fly line straight and not allowing any slack in the line. This is paramount for feeling a fish take your fly. The less slack in the line, the more often you can feel the take.

When retrieving the fly, don't overwork it. Yes, movement of the fibers on the fly is what entices a fish to eat, but overdoing it can turn fish away. As A. D. Livingston writes, "[M]erely following the natural drift of the current is sometimes the best possible way to work streamers and bucktails."[11] In other words, dead drifting a fly through a fishy-looking pocket could be enough to cause a fish to strike.

Another important technique when retrieving the fly is working it low and slow. Texas Hill Country fly fishing guide and author Kevin Hutchinson addresses this in *Fly Fishing the Texas Hill Country*: "Here your watch words should be low and slow… Fishing your flies deeper will yield more and bigger fish… If the number of calories gained by eating something outweighs the number of calories burned eating it, they will feed: it's simple math. If your fly is moving too fast, the math doesn't work out, so slow down."[12]

The last important facet to small-stream fishing is the need for stealth. Wary fish can easily spot a dangerous and shadowy creature looming over them, and they will make their escape into the nearest hidey-hole. When possible, cast into slow-flowing pools from a distance, and move through the water slowly. When approaching a fishy-looking section of water, stay low. Fish can only see above the water line at a 97-degree angle. This is because of a phenomenon called Snell's window. To clarify, think about how humans view the world. We can see 180 degrees, from one horizon to the other. But fish can only see above the waterline through a cone of 97 degrees. Anything outside of that cone is either distorted or reflected back into the subsurface of the water. This is due to refraction. The more agitated the surface of the water is, the less the fish can see above it.[13] Staying low when approaching a pool will keep you below Snell's window and thus distorted from the fish's view.

These are my personal techniques. You may already have developed your own techniques and strategies that work best for your style. The most important thing is to get out on the water and start fishing.

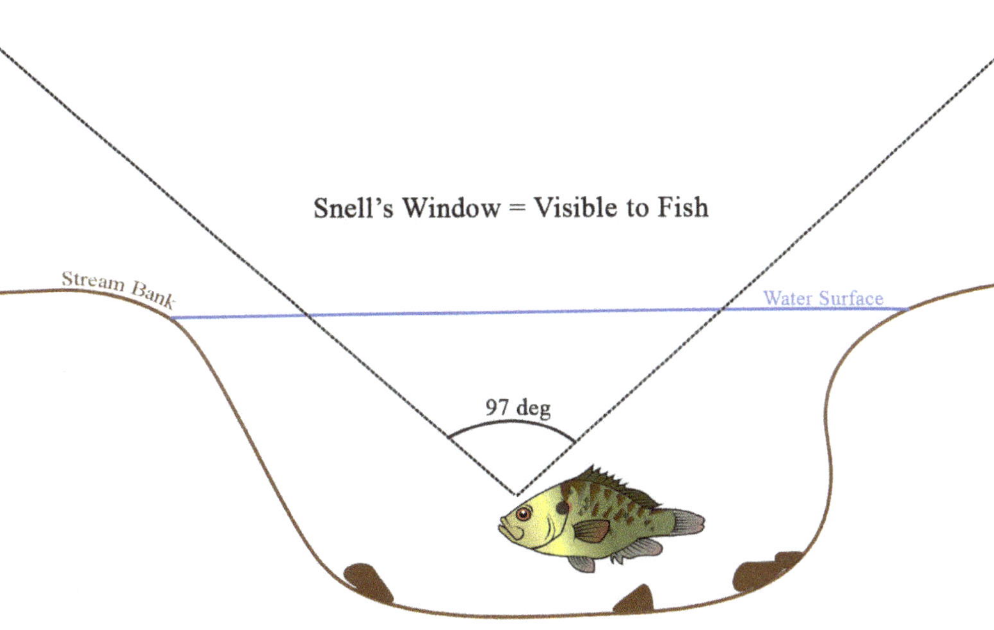

Fish handling

Proper fish handling techniques are vital to reduce injury and stress on fish. Abide by the #keepfishwet® principles.[14] Minimize the exposure of the fish to the air by landing the fish in the water and only holding it above the water for a short interval. Be sure to wet your hands before handling the fish. Try not to let the fish come in contact with dry surfaces. This will remove the protective layer of mucus on the fish's scales. Keep the gills in the water until your buddy is ready with the camera to snap that grip 'n' grin photo. Keep the fish over the water and support the body by placing a hand under the front fins. After the photo, promptly release the fish.

It is important to remember that you can cause injury to a bass if you hold the lower jaw cocked at a ninety-degree angle and let the weight of the body hang straight down. By "lipping" a large bass like this, you can dislocate the lower jaw. The proper handling technique is with two hands. One wet hand holds the lower jaw, keeping it aligned with the rest of the body, while the other wet hand supports the body.[15]

I almost always crimp the barbs on my hooks. I do this because the jaws of panfish can be fragile, and it is difficult to remove a barbed hook from the small mouth of a panfish without causing injury.

Drew Fletcher releases a spotted bass in the East Fork San Jacinto River.

Longear sunfish from East Sandy Creek

How to use this book

Each creek described in the following pages has certain symbols associated with it. This is to help the reader quickly gain a basic understanding of the fishery. The symbols denote three things: ease of access, ecological significance/quality, and the most common types of fish caught at the location.

Ease of access

Streams are awarded one, two, or three hiking boots to signify the ease with which the stream segment can be accessed and how difficult it is to walk the banks.

The hike to the water is short and on well-marked trails. Wading and hiking the stream is relatively easy.

The hike to the water can be upwards of half a mile across fairly easy terrain. Wading and walking the stream will require some bushwhacking.

The hike to the water is an adventure. There are no established trails, and the hike could be over a mile long. The undergrowth along the stream is dense and will require plenty of bushwhacking.

Ecological significance and water quality

Some waterways in the Sam Houston National Forest have been designated by the state of Texas as ecologically significant river and stream segments (ESRSS). This symbol means the Texas Water Development Board—along with input from the Texas Natural Resource Conservation Commission, the Texas Parks and Wildlife Department, the US Fish and Wildlife Service, two state universities, and several other agencies—has deemed the waterway to be ecologically unique and valuable to the state.[16] This designation is given on the basis of the following criteria:

A fine evening on the upper reaches of Winters Bayou

1. Biological Function – The stream segment is biologically diverse and exhibits quality habitat for aquatic and terrestrial organisms.
2. Hydrologic Function – The stream is bordered by important habitat that can serve as groundwater recharge, provide flood attenuation, and perform other important functions related to water resources.
3. Riparian Conservation Area – The stream is bordered by riparian areas that are owned by the general public and contribute to outdoor recreation, such as parks, wildlife management areas, and national forest lands.
4. Exceptional Water Quality and Aquatic Life – The stream is fed by spring water that exhibits exception water quality and contributes to the biodiversity of the stream.
5. Threatened or Endangered Species – The stream and/or adjacent riparian habitat contains threatened or endangered species.

Common types of sport fish caught on the fly

Types of sport fish will be displayed next to the name of the creek. Of course, this doesn't mean these are the only types of fish that live in the waterway. These are just commonly angled sport fishes that reside in the specified stream all year round. Specific varieties of panfish and bass will be described in more detail starting on page 58.

 Panfish

 Catfish

 Bass

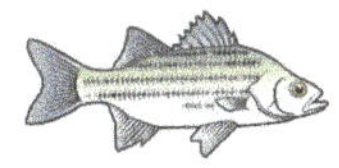 White bass

A shout-out to white bass

White bass spend most of their time in lakes, reservoirs, and large rivers. However, in early spring (February to April), these bass move upstream along tributaries and smaller waterbodies in order to spawn. While these fish make their run upstream, fly anglers can have a chance to catch them in the creeks, rivers, and bayous of the Sam. The white bass run is for avid Texas anglers what the steelhead run is for folks who live in the North. White bass are valuable as a sport fish but because they don't usually reside in the streams of the Sam year round, I opted not to focus on them in this work. With that being said, it is still possible to find them during the summer months in deep pools along the lower reaches of both the East Fork San Jacinto River and Winters Bayou (pages 50 to 53), but finding them is rare.

(Right)

White bass (*Morone chrysops*)

Lower reaches of the East Fork San Jacinto River

The Water

Overview

Winters Bayou and the East Fork of the San Jacinto River are the best waterways for fly fishing in the Sam Houston National Forest. It would take years to thoroughly explore them. At first glance, both Winters Bayou and the East Fork seem sluggish and murky. But I implore you, do not write them off. These are marvelous fisheries that truly exude a wilderness vibe. If you have limited time in the Houston area and are looking for a quick fly fishing fix, I recommend that you fish one of these two waterways. I'm sure that after several hours of exploring and fishing, you will see why they are so special.

Not only are the East Fork San Jacinto River and Winters Bayou loaded with fish, but they also hold historical significance to the state of Texas. The East Fork San Jacinto River was the easternmost boundary of Stephen F. Austin's colony, sometimes called the Old Three Hundred. Austin's father received a permit from the Spanish government to move approximately three hundred families of farmers from various parts of the Southern United States to the nutrient-rich bottomlands stretching from the Colorado River in the west to the East Fork San Jacinto River in the east. Austin's father died before the first settlers moved to the area, leaving Stephen to orchestrate the migration.[17]

Winters Bayou gets its name from a family of Tennesseans that migrated to Texas in 1834. They settled close to the banks of this bayou and quite possibly fished the same waters that we now fish—except they probably used homemade cane poles, not fancy fly rods. Two years after moving to East Texas, the Winters boys, along with other Texas volunteers, fought the Mexican army of Antonio López de Santa Anna at the Battle of San Jacinto on March 13, 1836. This was the concluding military engagement of the Texas Revolution and the deciding battle that granted independence to the Lone Star State. Today, the Winters family name lives on in the annals of history, as well as in the meandering waters of this tranquil bayou.[18, 19, 20]

James Washington Winters,

veteran of the Texas Revolution

(Dixon and Kemp, 1932)

Although Winters Bayou and the East Fork San Jacinto are the largest and most prolific fisheries within the Sam, there are still many other fantastic waterways that can be angled. The descriptions of these watercourses are organized geographically, starting on the western side of the Sam Houston National Forest and heading east.

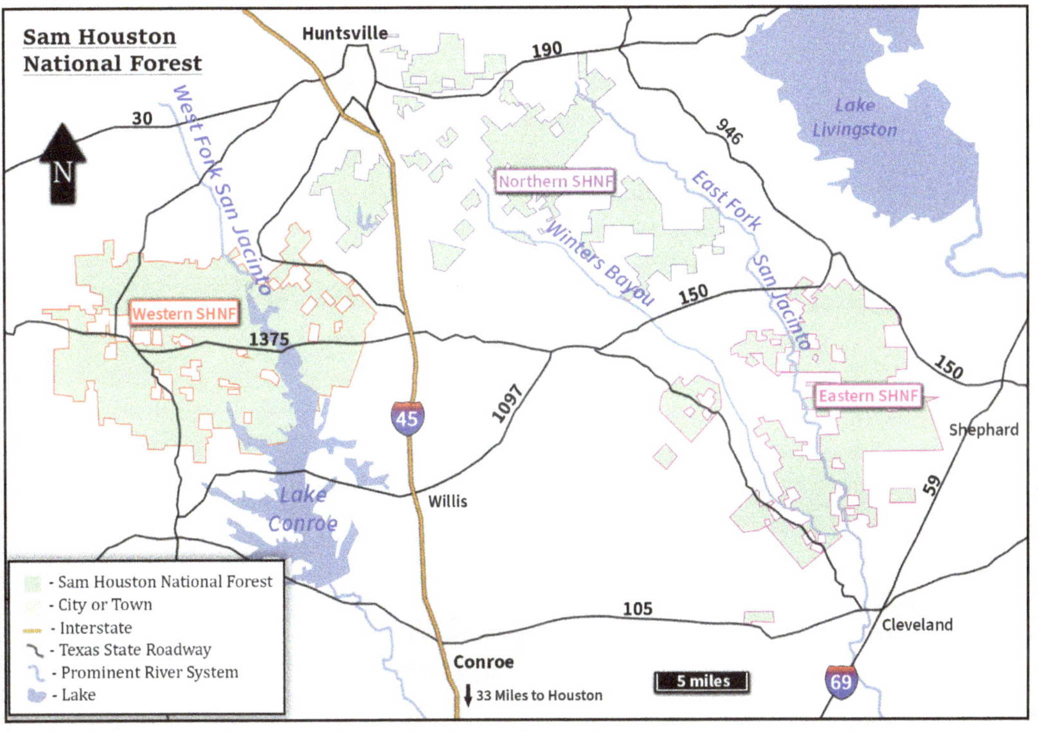

<u>(Above)</u>

Regional map showing the approximate location of the Sam Houston National Forest. For purposes of organizing the waterways described within this book, the national forest has been sectioned into three different areas: Western, Northern, and Eastern Sam Houston National Forest (SHNF). The following pages will address specific creeks within each of these three areas.

WESTERN SAM HOUSTON NATIONAL FOREST

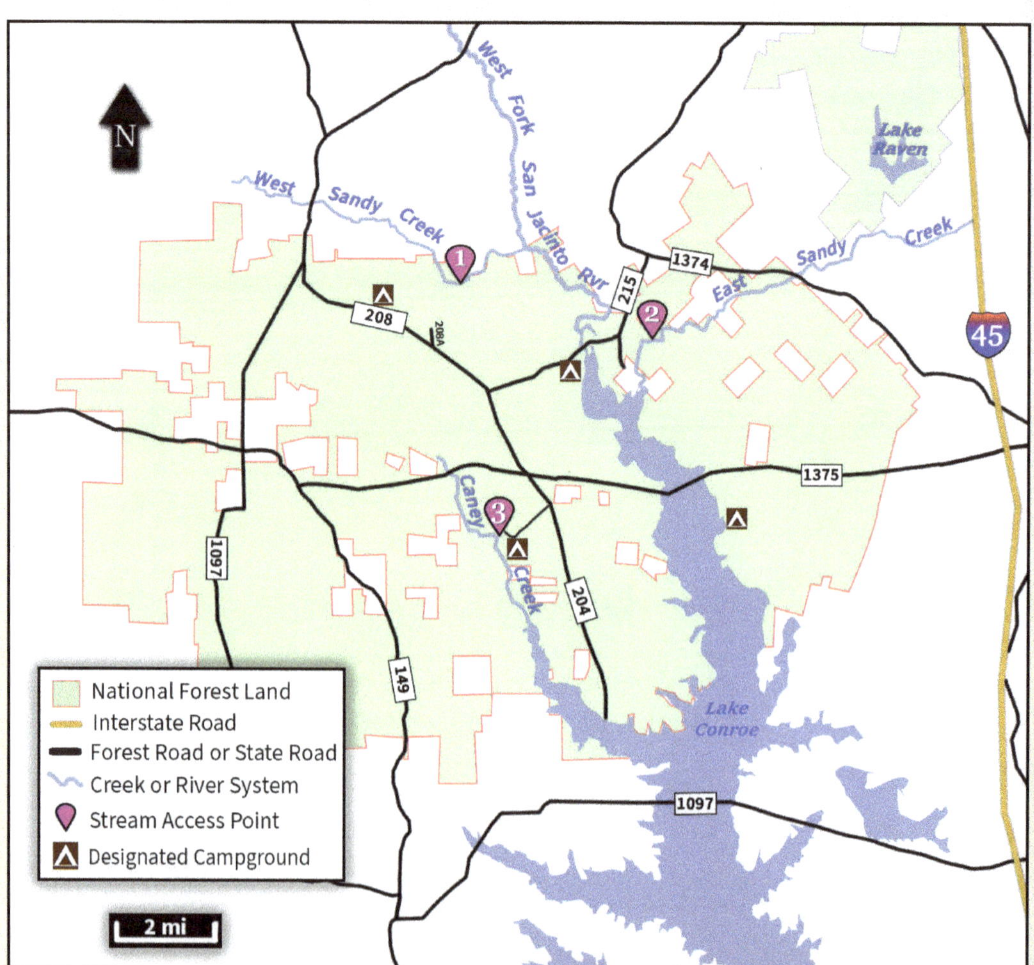

	Creek Name	Ease of Access	ESRSS Designation	Common Sportfish
1	**West Sandy Creek**		–	
2	**East Sandy Creek**		ESRSS	
3	**Caney Creek**		–	

West Sandy Creek

Creek Number	Ease of Access	ESRSS Designation	Common Sportfish
1		—	

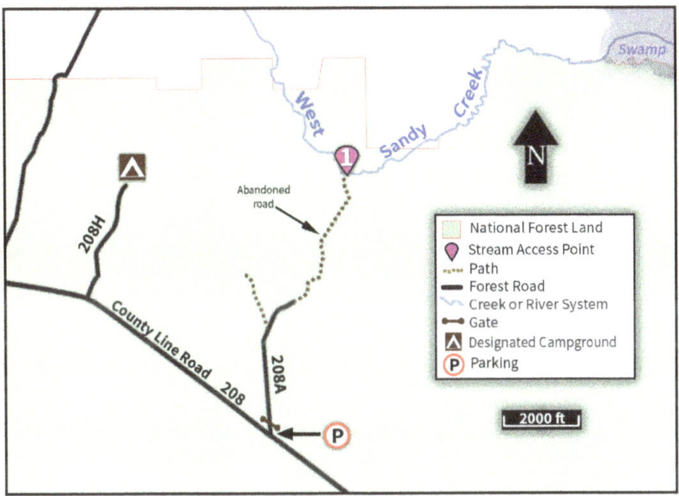

Parking QR Code

Access to West Sandy Creek

Park at the intersection of FS 208A and County Line Road, also known as FS 208 (30.56380 -95.68534). If the gate is closed, this is where you'll start a 1.4-mile trek. From the gate, hike approximately 800 yards to a Y inter-section. Stay right at this intersection and continue up a slight grade. You will eventually cross a large pipeline easement. At this point, the road is no longer maintained. Continue down the weed-choked road for .6 miles. You'll eventually come to a small field on the side of a gently sloping hill. Continue north, following the remnants of the road, to the banks of the West Sandy.

(RIGHT)

Longear hybrid from West Sandy

Characteristics of West Sandy Creek

If you can slog out the hike, West Sandy Creek can be a wonderful fishery for the pan-fish enthusiast. This creek has steep banks of mud and clay, with a bottom comprised mostly of mud and sand. The visibility into the water is around one foot. There are long, deep stretches of water that are confined within high banks. The banks can be as high as twelve feet in some areas, which makes it difficult to climb in and out of the stream. The flora surrounding the West Sandy is very dense. There are abundant canebrakes and palmettos along the creek. Be wary of the hardy orange bushes. These invasive plants were brought to Texas in the nineteenth century and were used along fencerows to keep livestock pastured. Take one look at the sizeable and vicious thorns on these shrubs, and you'll see why they were used as fencerows. Submerged plant matter and various woody debris is prevalent throughout the creek. Clambering over substantial logjams can be a chore, but it makes for excellent fish habitat. Unfortunately, litter is more prevalent in this creek than many other waterbodies addressed in this guide. Most of the trash appears to be old farm equipment and tires. Be mindful of the trash and watch where you step.

(TOP TO BOTTOM)

Sections of the West Sandy can be difficult to navigate, but finding a good hole full of panfish is worth the effort.

A small cascade is formed where West Sandy Creek flows over a log

Angling West Sandy Creek

A 3-weight is a good rod for fishing the healthy populations of panfish that inhabit this creek. Green sunfish, longear, warmouth, and bluegill are the most common. In addition to panfish, small bass can also be caught. The high creek banks keep the area above the water fairly devoid of overhanging limbs. This allows for longer casts. Most of the fish congregate in deep pools and along cut banks. Stripping flashy wet flies is a good strategy for most of this creek. As always, be sure to fish around the numerous logjams. Remember the mantra, "Wood is good."

A fiesty warmouth brought to hand on the West Sandy

(BELOW, LEFT)

Be careful of cottonmouths when moving along the banks of this creek. Sometimes they will be curled up in the logjams adjacent to the water.

(BELOW, RIGHT)

White crappie angled from a deep hole in West Sandy Creek

East Sandy Creek

Creek Number	Ease of Access	ESRSS Designation	Common Sportfish
2		ESRSS	

Parking QR Code

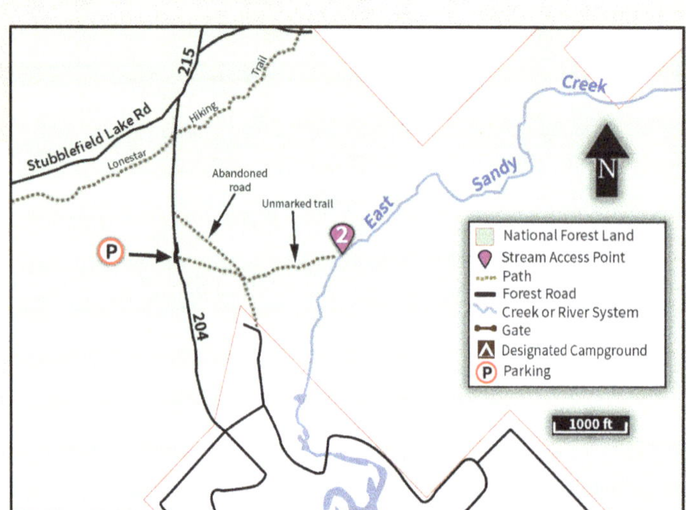

Access to East Sandy Creek

Park on either side of FS 204, also known as Gus Randel Road (30.56296, -95.62373). There is a pull-off adjacent to a power line. Look for a tree stump about four feet tall on the east side of the road. This is the trailhead to East Sandy Creek. The trail is very faint, so pay close attention as you hike into the creek. Continue southeast, down a slight grade into the creek bottom. Once in the bottomlands, the remnants of the trail disappear. Continue moving east through the dense undergrowth. You'll eventually come to the creek.

(RIGHT)

Sluggish lower section of
East Sandy Creek

Deep pools lead to swift flowing chutes on the upper sections of the East Sandy.

Characteristics of East Sandy Creek

This aesthetic watercourse runs through bottom-lands of large pines and hardwoods. The down-stream section of East Sandy Creek can be difficult to fish with a fly rod. The banks are high, muddy, and choked with vegetation, which limits access to the water. However, there are several sandy point bars along the lower reaches that provide fishing opportunities. As you move upstream, it becomes easier to access the water. The banks slope to the water's edge at a more gradual angle. There are plenty of logjams that make auspicious casting platforms as well. Along the upper reaches of East Sandy Creek, the banks and streambed transform into hard-packed clay and gravel bars. The water flows more swiftly through this upstream section. Visibility into the water can be anywhere from eight inches to one foot or more.

Longear sunfish from East Sandy Creek

Angling East Sandy Creek

As mentioned before, fly rodding the lower portion of this creek can be difficult. If you are able to access the water from one of the sandy point bars, then it is well worth fishing. Gar and redear sunfish patrol this slow-moving section of water. Along the swifter-flowing upper reaches, the water contains a healthy population of longear and bluegill. The various logjams and woody debris provide superb habitat for the diverse population of fish. In most cases, casts will need to be short to prevent overhanging vegetation from tangling the fly line. However, longer casts can still be made by standing in the middle of the stream. In the early spring, this stream can be a destination for anglers in pursuit of white bass.

A longear sunfish puts up a good fight on the East Sandy.

Working a wet fly around woody debris on the lower section of the East Sandy

Caney Creek

Creek Number	Ease of Access	ESRSS Designation	Common Sportfish
3		—	

Parking QR Code

Access to Caney Creek

Park at Kelly's Pond Campground (30.51058, -95.66312). This area is a designated hunter camp and is open to camping year-round. Caney Creek is approximately 400 yards southwest from the campground, but there is no defined trail to access the stream. Bushwhacking is the only way to get to the water from this location. Do not rig up the fly rod at the parking lot. A fully rigged fly rod could be broken in the dense thickets of cane and palmetto. Accessing and navigating this stream is challenging. Be prepared to crawl through brush and scramble over logs.

(RIGHT)

Most bass in Caney Creek are small. However, fighting small fish on lightweight tackle is very enjoyable.

Characteristics of Caney Creek

Much of Caney Creek is shrouded from the harsh rays of the sun by a dense canopy. Some sections of this tiny creek are so enveloped by vast entanglements of vines and cane that it feels as if the stream is flowing through a tunnel of impassable underbrush. The water has an amber hue, and clarity can be close to one foot. Accumulating sandbars create riffle sections that drop away into deep pools. Woody debris is prevalent throughout the creek, providing excellent habitat for an assortment of lotic creatures. During the late summer, the water flow is greatly diminished, but deep pools are still present.

Angling Caney Creek

Fishing Caney Creek is an adventure. Normally after fishing this waterway, you will leave with a sense of blissful accomplishment, but sometimes this temperamental creek can make you curse at the heavens in frustration. The secretive essence of this tiny waterway is what makes it a delight to fish, but be prepared to sweat and possibly bleed (just a little bit). Short roll casts and bow-and-arrow casts will be used regularly when

A chunky bluegill from Caney Creek

fishing this creek. In most cases, shallow sections can be by-passed. These shallow areas often flow into deep pools, so be sure to approach these pools slowly. If you go thundering through the water like a sounder of wild pigs, you'll surely spook the wary fish. In pools that contain an abundance of woody debris, you will find bluegills, green sunfish, and bass. Longear sunfish can be found in shallow runs and also in deep sections of the creek. Carp flies, like Danny Scarborough's Brasshawk, can be stripped along the bottom of the pools. This is a great way to pick up any bass feeding along the streambed. After the cast, remember to keep a little tension on the line while the fly sinks. That way, you can feel the tug on the line if a fish should strike the sinking fly. In late summer, when the water flow is diminished, concentrate on large, deep pools. The farther downstream you go, the more water you'll find.

Caney Creek downstream from Kelly's Pond Campground

Longear sunfish from Caney Creek

NORTHERN SAM HOUSTON NATIONAL FOREST

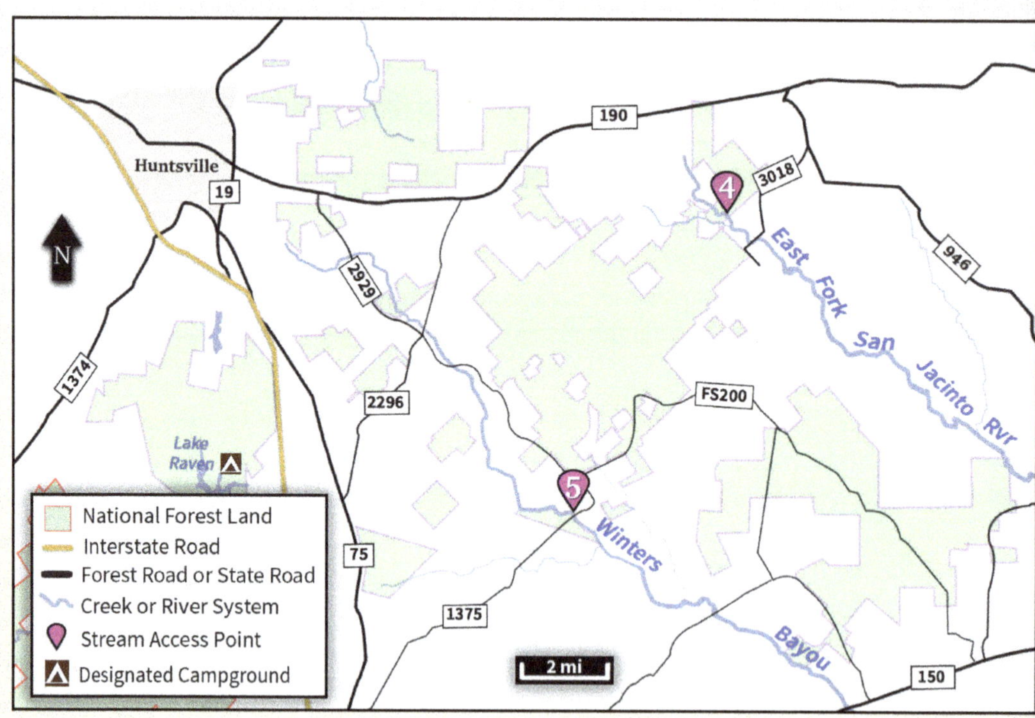

	Creek Name	Ease of Access	ESRSS Designation	Common Sportfish
4	**East Fork San Jacinto River – Upper Reaches**		ESRSS	
5	**Winters Bayou – Upper Reaches**		ESRSS	

East Fork San Jacinto River - Upper Reaches

Creek Number	Ease of Access	ESRSS Designation	Common Sportfish
4		ESRSS	

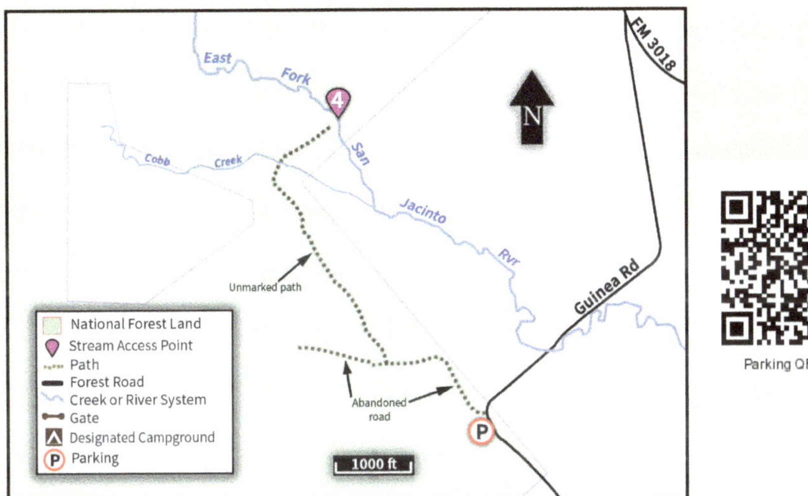

Parking QR Code

Access to East Fork San Jacinto River - Upper Reaches

Gaining access to this section of water is an adventure unto itself. Head southwest on FM 3018. Be on the lookout for a gravel road leading directly south called Guinea Road (30.70387, -95.32637). Follow Guinea Road through several pastures. The road will cross the East Fork San Jacinto. Do not fish here; both sides of the road are privately owned. Continue driving until you enter the tree line and no longer see the "No Trespassing" signs or the purple paint that denotes private property. Park on the shoulder of the gravel road (30.69050, -95.33237).

Now it's time to lace up your hiking boots. There is not a defined trail leading to this section of the East Fork San Jacinto. You must pay close attention to your surroundings as you bushwhack toward the waterway. Head northwest from the road, being careful not to enter the private property to the east. After hiking for roughly .79 miles, you will come to Cobb Creek. Cross this creek and hike another .3 miles to the upper reaches of the East Fork San Jacinto.

Characteristics of East Fork San Jacinto River - Upper Reaches

Once you finish bushwhacking through the hardwood bottomlands, you will come to a small waterway. This section of the East Fork San Jacinto is very close to the headwaters. Water clarity is around two to three feet. The clear water flows over a sandy-bottomed streambed. Gravel bars are numerous at riffle sections. The banks are low, and the water can be easily waded. Logjams and gravel bars create numerous pools. The exposed roots from large trees that line the banks make excellent habitat for numerous panfish species.

(ABOVE)

Warmouth from the upper reaches of East Fork San Jacinto

Making a stealthy cast on the upper reaches of the East Fork San Jacinto

Angling East Fork San Jacinto River - Upper Reaches

In this section of the East Fork, most of the fish are small, making a 3-weight rod an excellent choice. A tall canopy of sweetgum, oak, and pine keep most of the undergrowth at bay. Long casts can be accomplished with relative ease. Bluegills and longears are common, as well as green sunfish and warmouths. When approaching a pool, remember to stay low, below Snell's window (see page 19). Cast first to the edge of the pool closest to you before moving to the head of the pool, where the water flows in. Keep false casts to a minimum to avoid spooking the fish. If you're fishing this section in the summertime, be watchful of cottonmouths. They seem particularly fond of this portion of the East Fork. This is probably because of the clear water and abundance of fish. Check for these venomous serpents along logjams and gravel bars.

Winters Bayou - Upper Reaches

Creek Number	Ease of Access	ESRSS Designation	Common Sportfish
 5	👢	ESRSS	🐟🐟

Parking QR Code

Access to Winters Bayou - Upper Reaches

Park along the large shoulder of FM 1375 (30.60333, -95.40034). Winters Bayou flows under the road northeast of the aforementioned coordinates.

Clear and shallow section of the upper reaches of Winters Bayou, northwest of FM 1375

Characteristics of Winters Bayou - Upper Reaches

This section of Winters Bayou can be split into two unique stream segments. In the segment upstream (northwest of the road), the bayou flows at a different pace than the section downstream (southeast of the road). The upstream section appears to have more flowing water, and the streambed is mainly composed of sand. Riffle sections are created from numerous gravel bars. The upstream portion exhibits fantastic water clarity. This upstream section is heavily vegetated on both banks. The banks are fairly steep, which makes the easiest way of traveling simply walking the middle of the streambed.

Small bass from Winters Bayou

Small bluegill with striking colors

Upper reaches of Winters Bayou, southeast of FM 1375

Downstream of FM 1375, the flow of the water slows considerably and is often blocked by logjams or mudbanks, almost becoming stagnant in some sections. Water clarity through this portion of the bayou is poor. The streambed and steep, slippery banks are composed of mud, which contributes to the abundance of silt in the water. The trees are much taller here, which cuts down on the amount of underbrush and allows for longer casts.

Angling Winters Bayou - Upper Reaches

The upper reaches of Winters Bayou can be fished with a 3-weight. Most of the fish are panfish, although you will catch the occasional small bass. The prevalence of panfish species varies between the clear, upstream section (northwest of FM 1375) and the muddy, slow-flowing downstream (southeastern) section. There are plentiful green sunfish upstream of the road, but surprisingly, I haven't caught a single greenie downstream of FM 1375. Both above and below the road, bluegills and longears appear to be the most common panfish. I've also caught bass above and below the road. Fishing a dry fly or popper in the upstream section can be a fun and productive way to catch the greenies that inhabit this segment of the bayou. Fishing dry flies below the road doesn't appear to be productive, owing to the lack of water clarity. This section of Winters Bayou is another fantastic fishery for someone looking to catch panfish on the fly. The diverse population of sunnies make this area well worth fishing.

Deep pools are formed by logjams along the upper reaches of Winters Bayou.

If you fish this section of Winters Bayou, you'll undoubtedly notice the small lake just south of FM 1375. This is known as Walker Lake. While this lake can be a great place to make a couple of casts from the shore, it is best to fish this area using some kind of watercraft. All manner of fish inhabit this lake, including gar, bass, and various panfish species.

EASTERN SAM HOUSTON NATIONAL FOREST

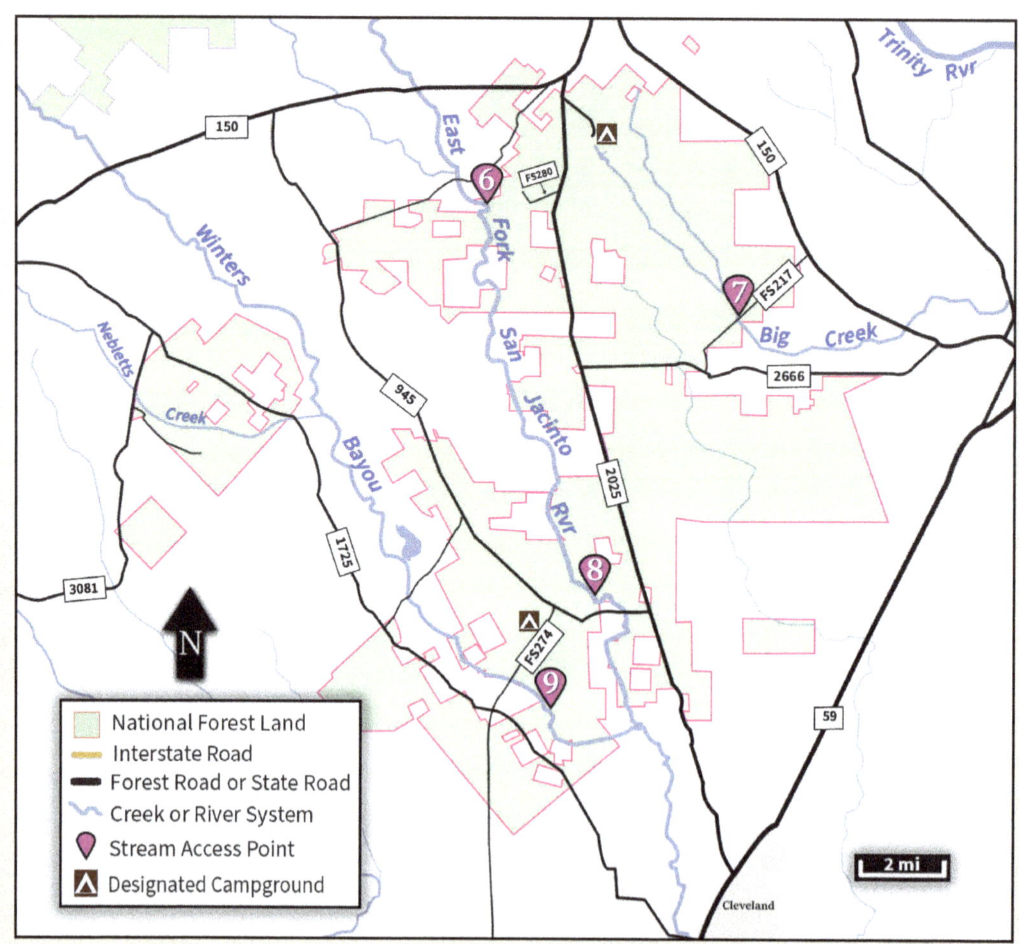

	Creek Name	Ease of Access	ESRSS Designation	Common Sportfish
6	**East Fork San Jacinto River - Middle Reaches**		ESRSS	
7	**Big Creek**		ESRSS	
8	**East Fork San Jacinto River - Lower Reaches**		ESRSS	
9	**Winters Bayou - Lower Reaches**		ESRSS	

East Fork San Jacinto River - Middle Reaches

Creek Number	Ease of Access	ESRSS Designation	Common Sportfish
6		ESRSS	

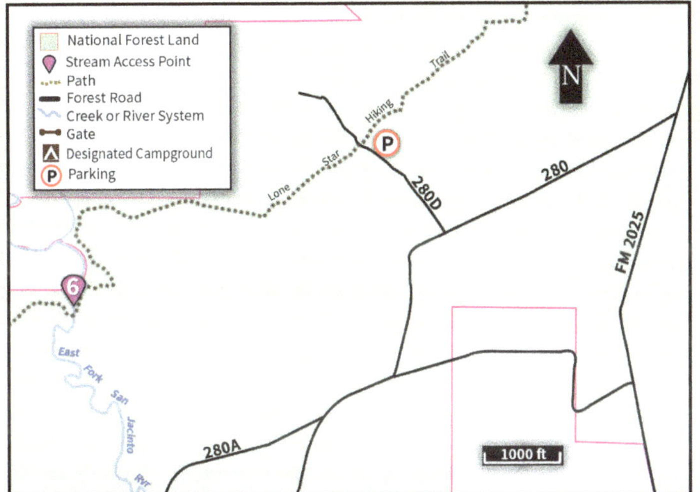

Parking QR Code

Access to East Fork San Jacinto River - Middle Reaches

From FM 2025, turn onto FS 280 (30.53984, -95.14576) and head southwest. This gravel road will lead into the Coldspring Oil Field. The first road on the right will be FS 280D (30.53620, -95.15515). Make this right and continue on until a power line crosses the road (30.53910, -95.15828). Park near the power line. Walk the gravel road, heading northwest, to the intersection of the Lone Star Hiking Trail. Take the hiking trail west for 1.1 miles. This section of trail is well maintained and enjoyable to hike. Hike until the trail crosses the East Fork San Jacinto.

Middle reaches of East Fork San Jac

Characteristics of East Fork San Jacinto River - Middle Reaches

The middle section of the East Fork San Jacinto River slowly worms its way through gently rolling bottomlands. The murky water flows along steep muddy banks. Visibility can be anywhere from a couple of inches to one foot depending on turbidity. Be careful, as the banks are slippery in some areas. In some places, the streambed can be very soft. If you find yourself getting sucked into the mud, move slowly and watch your footing. Woody debris is prevalent throughout this section of the East Fork. This makes great habitat for fish, but can also be a tripping hazard to the unwary angler.

(LEFT TO RIGHT)

A bass angled from the middle reaches of the East Fork San Jacinto

A typical bluegill from the middle reaches of the East Fork San Jacinto

Angling East Fork San Jacinto River - Middle Reaches

Don't let the muddled water deter you from fishing this section of the East Fork. The number of fish and variety of species make this section well worth angling. Using flashy flies is a good strategy. The silty water is wide enough for longer casts, but you should still be cautious of low-hanging branches. Cast toward sunken logs, especially in deep holes. Strip the fly parallel to the side of the log. Bass and several species of panfish are lurking under these drowned arboreal hideaways. A 5-weight rod is a good choice when fishing this water. A 5-weight will permit an enjoyable fight with smaller panfish but also have enough backbone to handle a bass when it ambushes your fly.

(ABOVE)

Spawning longear sunfish often exhibit striking colors. Bringing a brightly colored longear to hand is one of the greatest joys of fly fishing the Sam. This fish was angled from the middle reaches of the East Fork San Jacinto River.

Big Creek

Creek Number	Ease of Access	ESRSS Designation	Common Sportfish

Parking QR Code

Access to Big Creek

Park at the Big Creek Scenic Area (30.50588, -95.08880). This is off of FS 217. This area has a myriad of hiking trails that grant easy access to Big Creek. Another great place to start fishing is right off FS 217. Continue to follow the road east, out of the parking lot, until it crosses the water. Here a natural dam has formed on the south side of the road, creating a pond.

Big Creek

Characteristics of Big Creek

Of all the creeks and streams flowing through the Sam Houston National Forest, this is one of the most picturesque. Big Creek begins at the confluence of Henry Lake Branch and Double Lake Branch. The former is responsible for contributing most of the water to the Big Creek system. This unique waterway weaves its way through gently rolling terrain. Its waters are shrouded in a thick canopy of large trees. Some sections of the water flow through open marshy areas. Thick grasses and reeds grow on either side of the bank. This change in surrounding habitat leads to diversity in aquatic life. The water clarity is excellent; visibility extends three feet or more. The substrate of the creek is primarily sand with some gravel bars present at shallow riffles. Riffle sections flow into clear pools or deep cut banks. In some areas, small shrubs and trees skirt the banks, which can make it difficult to cast.

(RIGHT)

Hybridized panfish species are a common sight in Big Creek. This is due to the diversity of panfish species that inhabit this water.

Angling Big Creek

Most fish in this waterway are panfish. An ultralight rod, such as a 2- to 3-weight, is a great choice for angling this creek. Redbreast sunfish abound in these waters. Their feisty nature and voracious appetite make them an absolute blast to fish with lightweight gear. In addition to the redbreast sunfish, this diverse creek holds longears, bluegills, redspotted sunfish, and the occasional bass. Due to the size of this creek, the bass are fairly small. Most riffles and shallow runs can be ignored by the angler; these areas are often too shallow to hold fish. Concentrate on deeper pools and cut banks, especially where flowing currents have exposed the roots of nearby trees. Some parts of this waterway will seem too shallow and tight to fish. If you run across a section of water like this, simply move upstream. Chances are you'll find a wider and deeper pool. You never know what is going to bend the rod in this waterway. I've caught small bass in one pool and redbreast sunfish, longears, and redspotted sunfish in the next. The diversity of fish in this creek should be held in high regard.

East Fork San Jacinto River - Lower Reaches

Creek Number	Ease of Access	ESRSS Designation	Common Sportfish
 8		ESRSS	

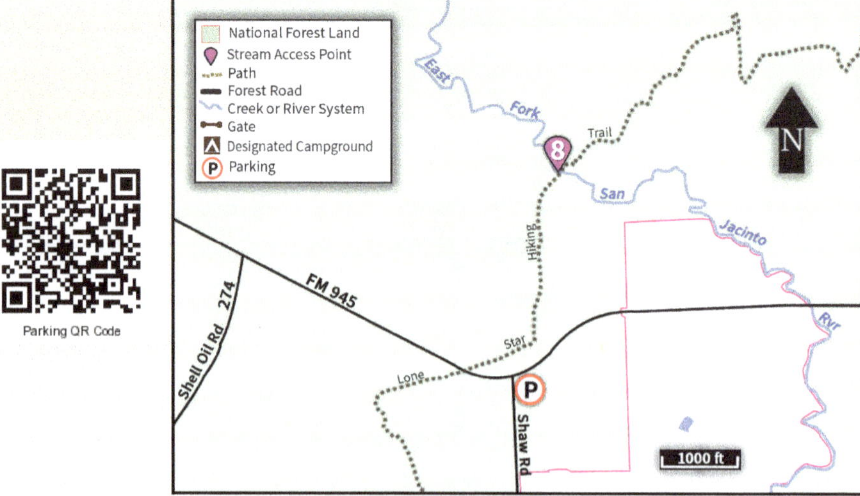

Parking QR Code

Access to East Fork San Jacinto River - Lower Reaches

Park at the pull-off at the intersection of Shaw Road and FM 945 (30.42259, -95.13671). The Lone Star Hiking Trail crosses FM 945 just west of this intersection. Take the hiking trail northeast, through the pines, for .6 miles. A large metal bridge spans the East Fork of the San Jacinto. Scramble down the bank and hit the water.

Healthy spotted bass from the lower reaches of the East Fork San Jacinto

Will Baxter drifts a fly around sunken logs on the lower reaches of the East Fork San Jacinto.

Characteristics of East Fork San Jacinto River - Lower Reaches

This section of the East Fork San Jacinto is a majestic wilderness. A towering forest casts a shadowy veil over this small river. The sandy riverbed is wide enough for longer casts, and most of the river can be waded. The abundance of sunken logs creates great lotic habitat for bass and panfish. Sloughs and small braided off-chutes offer countless opportunities to explore curious-looking waters. Most days, visibility is around one foot. On days when the flow is low, the water is surprisingly clear, usually enough to see two feet or more into the still pools. There are signs of river otters on many of the point bars. Be on the lookout for their scat and tracks. You might even be lucky enough to see one. Their presence is a testament to the abundance of aquatic forage in this waterway.

(Right)

Adam Samale with a spotted bass, lower reaches of the East Fork San Jacinto River

The Water   51

Angling East Fork San Jacinto River - Lower Reaches

Some of the panfish species that I have angled in this section of the East Fork include longears, bluegills, redspotted sunnies, and warmouths. While catching one of these feisty and beautiful fish is worth the hike, the real prize is catching one of the voracious spotted or largemouth bass that inhabit this section of the river. I venture to say that a 5-weight is plenty of rod for this water. I haven't found the bass to be trophy-sized—this is a fairly small waterway, after all—but you still want to have a beefy leader tied on. I recommend using at least 2X tippet. Spotted bass will almost always run for the cover of sunken trees, so you'll need a tippet strong enough to turn them away from their escape route. When fishing this section of water, be prepared to hook into channel catfish. When you see the fish on the end of your line barrelrolling toward the surface of the water, you'll know you caught a channel cat. This small river is ecologically diverse, and it provides ample fishing opportunities. It is a wonderful place to wet a line.

(LEFT)

Channel catfish angled from the lower reaches of the East Fork San Jacinto using Scarborough's Brasshawk carp fly

Winters Bayou - Lower Reaches

Creek Number	Ease of Access	ESRSS Designation	Common Sportfish
9		ESRSS	

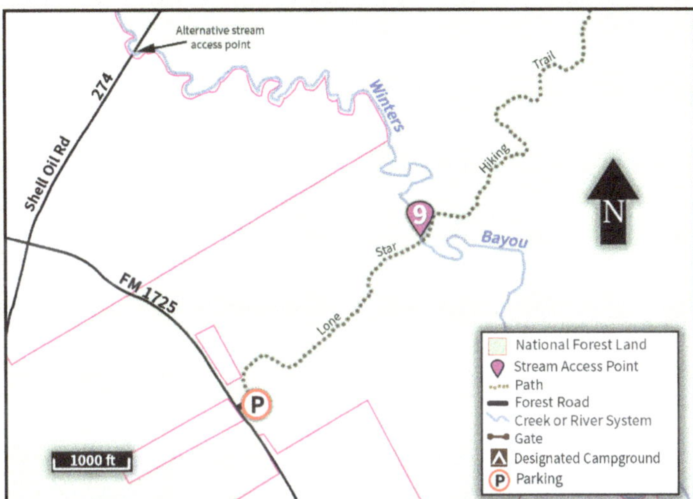

Parking QR Code

Access to Winters Bayou - Lower Reaches

Park at the Winters Bayou Scenic Area parking lot (30.39315, -95.15808). This is the trailhead for the Lone Star Hiking Trail. From the parking lot, head northeast along the trail. You'll hike through towering pines for .65 miles until you come to Winters Bayou. An impressive metal bridge spans the length of the waterway. It is easiest to access the water from the northern side of the bayou (river left).

(Right)

Large metal bridge spans Winters Bayou along the Lone Star Hiking Trail

Characteristics of Winters Bayou - Lower Reaches

This direct route to Winters Bayou will enable you to explore the downstream reaches of this watercourse. From here, it's about 3.2 river miles to the confluence of the East Fork of the San Jacinto River. Because this is the most downstream section, the water has had ample time to pick up fine sediments. This gives the water a muddy look. However, on days when the flow is low, water clarity can be anywhere from one to two feet. The color of the water is usually amber but sometimes carries a reddish hue. A low canopy of vegetation covers the length of this section of the bayou. The substrate of the bayou is primarily sand but gravel bars are present at many of the riffle sections. Root wads and logjams produce off-channel areas that serve as habitat for various aquatic critters.

(RIGHT)

Largemouth bass from the lower reaches of Winters Bayou

Kyle Hampton uses a log as a casting platform on Winters Bayou.

Angling Winters Bayou - Lower Reaches

In most areas, casts will need to be short. This is due to the low canopy of trees that envelopes the waterway. Longer casts can still be made from the middle of the water in some areas. Longear sunfish are common in pools and around woody debris in shallow runs. Oftentimes, a trough will be scoured from the sand just behind a sunken log. Stripping a small streamer through these troughs will often yield a beautiful longear.

Largemouth, spotted bass, and the occasional white bass can be found in deeper pools. Dead drifting a wet fly through a swift-flowing chute can be an excellent way to elicit a strike from a spotted bass waiting in ambush. Besides fishing typical streamer patterns, heavy carp flies can be stripped along the bottom of pools and along deep cut banks. Channel catfish can be caught using this method.

(LEFT TO RIGHT)

Spotted bass from Winters Bayou, caught in the month of December by fishing "slow and low" through a deep hole

A December evening on Winters Bayou

The Water   55

Ponds and Lakes of the Sam Houston National Forest

By simply using Google Earth and scanning the Sam Houston National Forest, you'll undoubtedly discover numerous ponds and small lakes. Some of these bodies of water are oxbow lakes from ancient river channels. Others are old farm ponds or dammed swamps. I won't go into detail on fishing specific ponds and lakes. I encourage you to strike out and find them on your own. If you find a pond within the Sam that holds a healthy population of fish, it can be a great place to angle if the creeks and rivers are too blown out from heavy rainfall.

There is one caveat worth mentioning: It is very difficult to fish many of the ponds from the shore. Often, the vegetation surrounding the pond is too thick and will prevent the angler from making long casts. Using some kind of watercraft is usually the best bet for having a successful day of fishing on one of the forest ponds. Using a canoe, kayak, or raft can allow access to the entire body of water.

Using a watercraft comes with its own set of challenges. Transporting the vessel to and from the water can be difficult. Especially if the pond requires a hike to get to it. You'll often need a recruit – preferable one that doesn't complain too much – to help lift and drag the watercraft to the secluded pond.

Angling Ponds and Lakes of the Sam

Ponds and lakes in the Sam are a great place to find bigger largemouth bass. Slow-moving, weed-choked waters are ideal habitat for largemouth. If frogs are abundant around the pond, try mimicking this food source by using topwater flies like poppers and gurglers.

If heavy rains have caused flooding conditions in the streams, don't let this stop you from getting out and fishing. The secluded ponds and lakes of the national forest can still be a great place to angle. You may even catch a monster bucketmouth. Gaining access to a pond can bring additional challenges, but it's often worth the effort.

Large lake in the Sam Houston National Forest

Spotted bass from the lower reaches of the East Fork San Jacinto River

The Fish

Fish Identification

The waters of the Sam Houston National Forest contain an impressive variety of fish. The following composite pictures will help fellow anglers identify the seven panfish species and two black bass species often found here. Panfish and black bass are the only types of fish included in this section because they are the most common sport fish in the Sam.

Only fish that were angled from the waters of the Sam Houston National Forest are included in the following images. By doing this, I hope to show the reader the specific color variations and morphology that exist in the area.

Most of the species characteristics described in the following pages come from *Peterson Field Guide to Freshwater Fishes*, second edition, by Lawrence M. Page and Brooks M. Burr.[21] This book is an invaluable resource to anyone interested in fish identification. I highly recommend it to anyone who fishes the freshwater lakes, streams, and rivers of North America.

Panfishes (*Lepomis*) 

I didn't give much credence to panfish (the *Lepomis* genus) as a sport fish until I started fly fishing the Sam. Since then, I have developed an affinity for them. Morphology of panfish vary based on their environment, and they sometimes hybridize. These factors can make them difficult to identify. The composite images on the following pages should help the angler make positive identifications of the panfish species that live in the Sam Houston National Forest.

Bluegill

Warmouth

Green sunfish

Redbreast sunfish

Bluegill (*Lepomis macrochirus*)

Characteristics: Two blue streaks extend from the chin to the edge of the gill plate. Olive coloring along the dorsal area. White to yellow color along belly. On adults, a large black spot can be seen toward the rear of the dorsal fin. In clear waters, dark vertical bars extend down from the back and over the side of the body. These bars are greatly diminished in murky waters. Pectoral fin is long, extending past the eye when bent forward. Ear flap is black and can be fairly long on adults. Mouth is small. Upper jaw doesn't extend to the front of the eye. Can grow to 16.25 inches. (Page and Burr, 2011: 502)

Author's Note: Bluegills are a common fish throughout the Sam Houston National Forest. They don't grow to epic proportions like you might see in farm ponds or large lakes. Nonetheless, they are still fun to catch. They are often found in schools. When you catch one, be prepared to catch many more.

Green Sunfish (*Lepomis cyanellus*)

Characteristics: A large mouth with the upper jaw extending under the eye. Blue-green, wormlike markings around eyes and cheeks. Dorsal, pelvic, anal, and caudal fins usually have yellowish edges. Adults have a dark spot at the base of the dorsal and anal fins. Back is usually blue to green in color. Belly is usually yellow. Ear flap is short and stiff with a black spot. The edge of the ear flap is often yellow on adults. Pectoral fins are short, rarely reaching the eye when bent forward. Can grow to 12 inches. (Page and Burr, 2011: 500)

According to Texas Parks and Wildlife, these sunfish are one of the state's hardiest sunfish species. They can tolerate wild swings in environmental conditions.[22]

Author's Note: I have an affinity for greenies. They are strong fighters on the fly rod, and because they are often found in schools, hooking into one will tell you that there are more nearby. Their large mouths allow them to take bigger flies, and they will readily hit topwater flies.

Longear Sunfish (*Lepomis megalotis*)

Characteristics: Long ear flap is horizontal or pointed slightly downward on adults. Adults usually have a thin pale line around the edge of the ear flap. Wavy and wormlike blue markings on cheeks, extending back over the gill plate. Bright red coloring along the back and reddish orange along the belly. Sides are colored blue to green. Pectoral fins are short, usually not reaching past the eye when bent forward. Mouth is large. Upper jaw extends under the front of the eye when mouth is closed. Can grow to 9.5 inches. (Page and Burr, 2011: 504)

Longears closely resemble another sunfish called a dollar sunfish (*Lepomis maginatus*). However, because dollar sunfish only grow to be a maximum of 4.75 inches, they aren't often hooked on larger flies. If you are fishing a swampy area and catch a fish that resembles a minature longear with blue markings across its ear flap instead of the usual black, it's probably a dollar sunfish. (Page and Burr, 2011: 506)

Author's Note: Longear sunfish are commonly found in the streams, rivers, and bayous of the Sam Houston National Forest. Their vibrant colors place them among the most beautiful of freshwater fish. They are small, but have a big attitude.

Redbreast Sunfish (*Lepomis auritus*)

Characteristics: Black ear flap is long and narrow, extending midway down the body. Wormlike blue markings extend from the edge of the mouth and over the gill plate. Belly is bright yellow to orange in color. Mouth is fairly large. Upper jaw extends under the front edge of the eye. Can grow to 9.5 inches. (Page and Burr, 2011: 506) Redbreast sunfish, sometimes referred to as "yellow bellies," are one of the largest sunfish species in Texas. Some specimens can weigh as much as one pound.[23]

Author's Note: Redbreast sunfish are not native to Texas. Nevertheless, they are an excellent sport fish. They attack flies with tenacity and put up a good fight when hooked. I'm often surprised at their large size, especially considering the small waterbodies in which I find them.

Redear Sunfish (*Lepomis microlophus*)

Characteristics: Bright red-orange edge on ear flap, directly behind large black dot. Pectoral fins are long and pointed, reaching to the eye or past it when bent forward. Mouth is small and face is quite pointed. The upper jaw does not extend under the eye. Light golden green back and yellowish white belly. Can grow to 10 inches. (Page and Burr, 2011: 503)

According to Texas Parks and Wildlife, these sunfish are native to the eastern side of the state. However, they have been introduced to other parts of Texas. These fish reside near the bottom of slow-flowing bodies of water. They have an affinity for aquatic snails and therefore are sometimes called "shellcrackers." Redears can be difficult to angle on the fly rod because they rarely approach the surface of the water.[24]

Author's Note: I haven't caught many redears in the Sam Houston National Forest. They are somewhat of a mystery to me. The few I have caught were hooked in deep water. Bouncing carp flies and nymphs along the bottom of a slow-moving section of water appears to be the most productive way to catch these panfish.

"

Redspotted Sunfish (*Lepomis miniatus*)

Characteristics: The redspotted sunfish has rows of red to yellow spots along the sides and a red-orange area above the ear flap. Pectoral fins are short, not reaching past the eye when bent forward. Rear edge of gill cover is stiff, with a short black ear flap. Area around mouth and cheeks lacks the wormlike blue markings of longear sunfish. Can grow to 8 inches. (Page and Burr, 2011: 501)

These small sunfish can be found in heavily vegetated pools and deep chutes. Much of their diet consists of aquatic invertebrates found along streambeds.[25]

Redspotted sunfish can be confused for the smaller bantam sunfish, *Lepomis symmetricus*. However, bantam sunfish lack the reddish spot above the ear flap as well as the rows of red spots along their sides.

Author's Note: I can count on one hand the number of times I have hooked into a redspotted sunfish while fishing the Sam. They are small, but incredibly beautiful. I consider these fish to be the hidden gems of the Sam Houston National Forest. When you catch one, be sure to examine its dark red spots and eyes. Once you hold one in your hand, I'm sure you'll see why they are a treasured fish.

Warmouth (*Lepomis gulosus*)

Characteristics: Large mouth. Upper jaw extends well under pupil when the mouth is closed. Brown to black lines radiate back from the eye. Pectoral fins are usually rounded and short, not extending to the eye when bent forward. The short stiff ear flap is marked with a black dot. Adults have a small red or yellow dot on the edge of the ear flap. Body is well camouflaged. Brown to olive bars extend from the back and down the sides. The belly is often yellow. Can grow to 12 inches. (Page and Burr, 2011: 498) These solitary ambush predators can usually be found in sluggish streams with muddy substrates. Their diet consists of a wide variety of aquatic species, including crayfish and minnows. Warmouth are crepuscular by nature and are least active during midday.[26][27]

Author's Note: The warmouth may look like a drab fish, but catching one of these feisty sunfish is anything but dull. Because of their large mouth, they often eat flies that are too big for them. They are ambush predators, so cast toward heavily vegetated areas with plenty of cover. Any day that a warmouth is brought to hand should be considered a great day of fly fishing.

Black Basses (*Micropterus*) 

The streams of the Sam Houston National Forest are home to two species of black basses: spotted bass and largemouth bass. At first glance, these distinct species appear very similar. This can lead to confusion and misidentification. The following descriptions and pictures should help anglers decipher the difference between spotted bass and largemouth bass. The bass that appear in the following photographs were caught in the waters of the Sam Houston National Forest.

Kyle Hampton prepares to release a spotted bass back into the waters of Winters Bayou.

Largemouth Bass (*Micropterus salmoides*)

Characteristics: Very large mouth. When mouth is closed, the upper jaw extends well past the back of the eye. The first dorsal fin is tallest in the middle, and usually appears to be disconnected from the second dorsal fin. A distinct black stripe runs the length of the fish, from head to base of the tail. Presence of this black lateral line is dependent on water clarity. Black line can be greatly diminished or absent in turbid water. Tongue is usually smooth to the touch. Prefers slow moving or still water with plenty of vegetation. Can grow to 38 inches. (Page and Burr, 2011: 493)

Largemouth bass are one of the largest aquatic predators found in the lotic environments of the Sam. Much like their cousins, the spotted bass, they ambush their prey. According to a study by Charles G. Scarlett (1977), the diet of the river-dwelling largemouth bass tends to consist mostly of fish. This is unlike the spotted bass, whose diet tends to be mostly crayfish.[28]

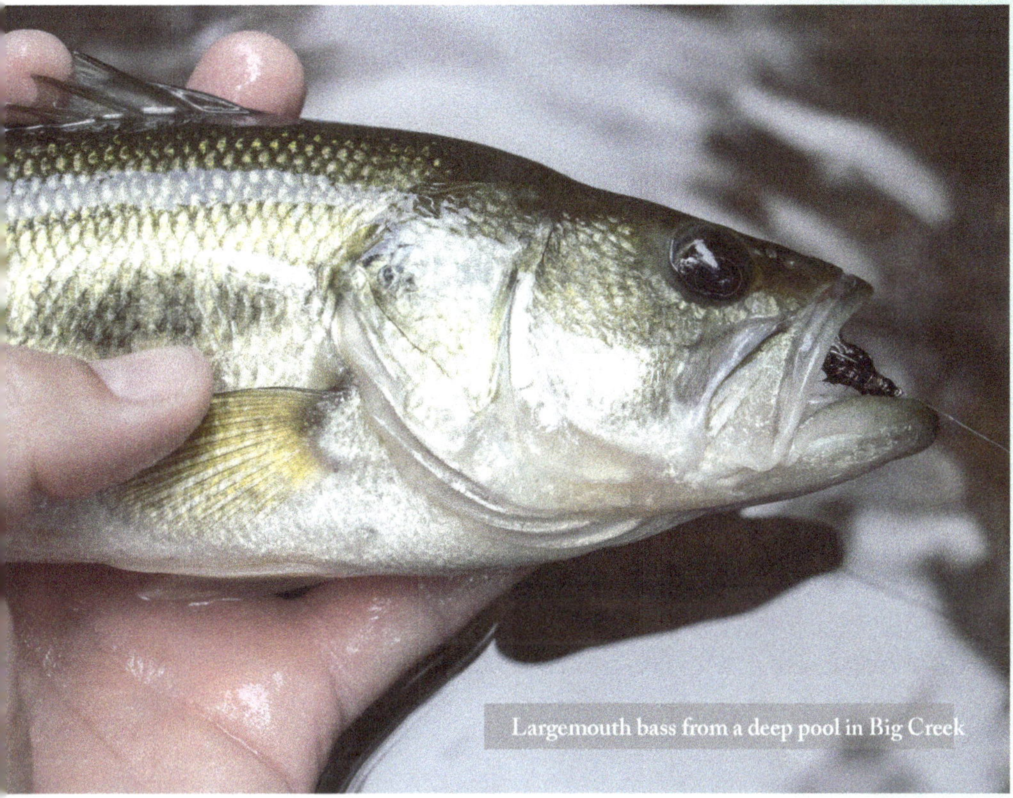

Largemouth bass from a deep pool in Big Creek

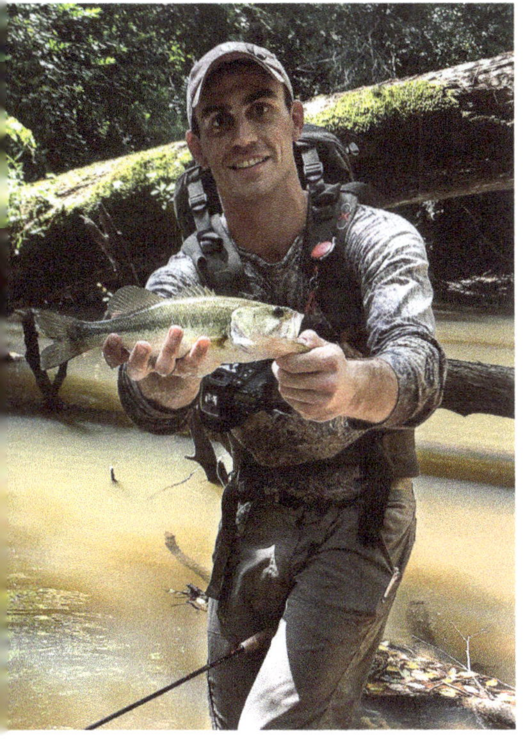

Author's Note: Largemouth bass can be found throughout the waterways of the Sam. You're more likely to catch them in deep and stagnant sections of water. The more weeds and vegetation are present, the more likely you'll find a largemouth.

(Photo credit: Will Baxter)

Spotted Bass (*Micropterus punctulatus*)

Characteristics: Fairly large mouth. When mouth is closed, the upper jaw extends under the eye, but not past it. First dorsal fin is tallest at the front and usually connects to the second dorsal fin. Small black spots on the sides and belly. Splotchy black lateral stripe. A black spot can sometimes be seen at the base of the tail (caudal area). The occurrence of distinct black markings is highly dependent on water clarity. The middle of the tongue is rough to the touch due to the presence of a "tooth patch." Often found in chutes and flowing pools in creeks and rivers. Can grow to 24 inches. (Page and Burr, 2011: 494)

Although these ambush predators feed on a wide variety of organisms, most of their diet consists of crayfish. Young spotted bass, usually 6 inches and smaller, supplement their diet with aquatic invertebrates. However, once the spotted bass grows larger than 8 inches, it feeds more heavily on small fishes along with its staple diet of crayfish.[29]

Nick Heaverlo with a spotted bass from the East Fork San Jacinto.

Author's Note: The spotted bass is the most common predator of the *Microp-terus* genus in the lotic environments of the Sam. These bass are an absolute blast to catch because they are found in small pools and chutes. In many cases, they act a lot like trout, living in pools and logjams in and around flowing currents. You'll be addicted to fly fishing the Sam after catching your first spotted bass. These green torpedoes will come speeding up from the depths of a shadowy chute and absolutely hammer your fly.

Longear sunfish

Conclusion

By now, I hope this book has successfully showcased the angling opportunities that exist in the streams, creeks, and bayous of the Sam Houston National Forest. This area is an important recreational resource for those who live in and around Houston. From a personal—and selfish—standpoint, I have thought for a long time about keeping this work a secret, like a personal fishing journal. But after much consideration, I would rather people use these words as inspiration to push deeper into the forest and do their own exploring. I hope people will find the same connection to this national forest that I have found. I acknowledge that fishing the wild bayous and streams of the Sam isn't for everyone. But it is my hope that this book will show my friends, colleagues, and fellow anglers that you don't need to get on a plane and fly to a faraway state for a wilderness fishing experience. You can accomplish it right here, within sixty miles of Houston.

There may be criticism from fellow anglers for publishing the locations of the previously mentioned waterways. Believe me, I understand this potential frustration, but I am convinced that bringing awareness to these diverse local fisheries is a good thing. We should take pride in the wild and beautiful waterways that exist so close to the city. With that being said, I won't lose a wink of sleep over this book, so long as it inspires someone to escape the urban landscape of cement and high-rises and wet a line somewhere in the Sam. Sometime in the future, I would love to sit down at the bar with fellow fly anglers, and instead of chatting about a fishing adventure in Wyoming or Montana, we could jaw about the big rowdy largemouth that we hooked in the East Fork of the San Jac. Houstonian fly fishermen should have pride in the streams of the Sam Houston National Forest. We should keep the waters clean and have respect for the fishery that exists so close to home. I sincerely hope that you will hike through the forests, explore the waterways, and fly fish the Sam.

Fly shops in the greater Houston area

Stop in at a fly shop before hitting the water. Here, local flies can be purchased and the knowledgable staff will help with any questions you may have.

Bayou City Angler
3641 Westheimer Rd. Houston, TX 77027
(832) 831-3104

Fishing Tackle Unlimited
10303 Katy Fwy. Houston, TX 77024
(713) 827-7762

Gordy & Sons, Outfitters
22 Waugh Dr. Houston, TX 77007
(713) 333-3474

Orvis, Woodlands
9595 Six Pines Dr. The Woodlands, TX 77380
(281) 203-6150

Craft breweries between Houston and the Sam

After a great day of fly fishing the Sam, stop in at one of these local breweries. Recalling the day's fishing exploits over a few frosty craft beers is a great way to end a successful fishing excursion.

Breweries in close proximity to RT-249:

Fire Ant Brewing Company
308 Market St. Tomball, TX 77375
(832) 720-7491

Lone Pint Brewery
507 Commerce St. Magnolia, TX 77355
(713) 304-5069

Breweries in close proximity to I-45:

B-52 Brewing Co.
12470 Milroy Ln. Conroe, TX 77304
(936) 447-4677

Copperhead Brewery
822 N Frazier St. Conroe, TX 77301
(281) 919-6134

Southern Star Brewing
3525 N Frazier St. Conroe, TX 77303
(936) 441-2739

Breweries in close proximity to I-69:

Back Pew Brewing Company
26452 Sorters McClellan Rd. Porter, TX 77365
(281) 608-7526

Megaton Brewery
808 Russell Palmer Rd. Kingwood, TX 77339
(281) 973-9043

Worthy Causes

Consider supporting the following organizations:

North American Native Fish Association

www.nanfa.org

NANFA is a 501(c)(3) non-profit corporation that promotes, conserves, and educates people on the importance of native fishes and their habitats. NANFA's focus encompasses all native fishes, down to the smallest minnows, shiners, darters, etc. The lively NANFA website and forum are an excellent place for discussions and education on all things related to fish. Visit their website to learn more.

Sam Houston Trails Coalition

www.samhoustontrails.org

The Sam Houston Trails Coalition is a 501(c)(3) non-profit dedicated to maintaining the many trails scattered throughout Sam Houston National Forest. This coalition not only maintains the hiking trails, but also the multi-use trails, equestrian trails, and motorized trails. This organization does a lot to keep the trails clear for all those who recreate in Houston's closest national forest.

Texas Streams Coalition

www.tx-streams.org

Texas Streams Coalition is a 501(c)(3) non-profit dedicated to conserving the habitat and wildlife within the rivers and streams of Texas, and protecting the rights of Texans to responsibly access those waters. TSC participates in river clean-up efforts, helps with outreach about waterway access rights, and promotes citizen science through water sampling and fish surveys.

Endnotes

1 Christopher Long, "Sam Houston National Forest," *Handbook of Texas Online*, http://www.tshaonline.org/handbook/online/articles/gks02.

2 "Principle 3: Dispose of Waste Properly," *Leave No Trace Center for Outdoor Ethics*, https://lnt.org/why/7-principles/dispose-of-waste-properly/.

3 "Freshwater Bag and Length Limits," *Texas Parks and Wildlife Outdoor Annual*, https://tpwd.texas.gov/regulations/outdoor-annual/fishing/freshwater-fishing/bag-length-limits.

4 United States Department of Agriculture Forest Service, *National Forests and Grasslands in Texas*, https://www.fs.usda.gov/texas.

5 Your Weather Service, *US Climate Data*, https://www.usclimatedata.com/climate/houston/texas/united-states/ustx0617.

6 *Ticks and Tick-Borne Diseases in Texas*, https://www.ticktexas.org/ticks/index_ticks.htm.

7 Steven Rinella, *The Complete Guide to Hunting, Butchering, and Cooking Wild Game, Volume 1: Big Game* (New York: Spiegel & Grau, 2015).

8 Danny Scarborough, "How to Tie a Brasshawk," *Houston Fly Fishing Guide Services*, https://www.houstonflyfishing.com/journal/2017/11/30/how-to-tie-a-brasshawk.

9 Terry Wilson and Roxanne Wilson, *The Bluegill Diaries: A Fly Fishing Chronicle* (Terry & Roxanne Wilson, 2017), 4.

10 A. D. Livingston, *Bass on the Fly* (Camden, ME: Ragged Mountain Press, 1994), 131-135.

11 Ibid.

12 Kevin Hutchinson, *Fly Fishing the Texas Hill Country* (Smithville, TX: Fishhead Press, 2008), 17.

13 David A. Ross, *The Fisherman's Ocean: How Marine Science Can Help You Find and Catch More Fish* (Mechanicsburg, PA: Stackpole Books, 2000), 150-152.

14 "Keepemwet Principles," *Keepemwet Fishing*, https://www.keepemwet.org/principles-2#principles.

15   "Trophy bass: Proper Catch-and-Release Handling Techniques," *Louisi
        ana Sportsman*, https://www.louisianasportsman.com/news-breaker/
        trophy-bass-proper-catch-and-release-handling-techniques/.

16   Chad W. Norris and Gordon W. Lineham, "Ecologically Significant River
        and Stream Segments – Region H," https://tpwd.texas.gov/publications/
        pwdpubs/pwd_rp_t3200_1059c/index.phtml.

17   "East Fork of the San Jacinto River," *The Handbook of Texas Online*,
        https://tshaonline.org/handbook/online/articles/rne06.

18   Thomas W. Cutrer, "Winters, James Washington, Jr.," *The Handbook of
        Texas Online*, https://tshaonline.org/handbook/online/articles/fwi66.

19   Andrew Jackson Sowell, *Early Settlers and Indian Fighters of Southwest
        Texas*, (Austin, TX: Ben C. Jones & Co Printers, 1900).

20   Sam Houston Dixon and Louis Wiltz Kemp, *The Heroes of San Jacinto*,
        (Houston, TX: The Anson Jones Press, 1932).

21   Lawrence M. Page and Brooks M. Burr, *Peterson Field Guide to Freshwater
        Fishes*, 2nd ed (New York: Houghton Mifflin Harcourt, 2011), 493-507.

22   Texas Parks and Wildlife, "Green Sunfish (*Lepomis cyanellus*)," https://
        tpwd.texas.gov/huntwild/wild/species/greensunfish/.

23   Texas Parks and Wildlife, "Redbreast Sunfish (*Lepomis auritus*)," https://
        tpwd.texas.gov/huntwild/wild/species/redbreastsunfish/.

24   Texas Parks and Wildlife, "Redear Sunfish (*Lepomis microlophus*)," https://
        tpwd.texas.gov/huntwild/wild/species/sunfish/.

25   Wayne J. Desselle, et al., "A discriminant functions analysis of
        sunfish (*Lepomis*) food habits and feeding niche segregation in the Lake
        Pontchartrain, Louisiana, estuary," *Transactions of the American Fisheries
        Society* 107, no. 5 (1978): 713-719.

26   Robert J. Edwards, "Ecological Profiles for Selected Stream-Dwelling
        Texas Freshwater Fishes," Texas Water Development Board, University of
        Texas-Pan American, Edinburg, TX, 1997.

27   Richard Weldon Larimore, "Ecological Life History of the Warmouth
        (Centrarchidae)," *Illinois Natural History Survey, Bulletin* 21, no. 1 (1957):
        1-83.

28   Ibid.

29   Charles G. Scalet, "Summer Food Habits of Sympatric Stream Popula-
tions of Spotted Bass, *Micropterus punctulatus*, and Largemouth Bass, *M. salmoides*, (Osteichthyes: Centrarchidae)." *The Southwestern Naturalist* 21, no. 4 (1977): 493-501.

Index of Waterways

Western Sam Houston National Forest — 28

West Sandy Creek — 29

East Sandy Creek — 32

Caney Creek — 35

Northern Sam Houston National Forest — 38

East Fork San Jacinto River - Upper Reaches — 39

Winters Bayou - Upper Reaches — 41

Eastern Sam Houston National Forest — 44

East Fork San Jacinto River - Middle Reaches — 45

Big Creek — 48

East Fork San Jacinto River - Lower Reaches — 50

Winters Bayou - Lower Reaches — 53

Species List

Panfish

		Page	Fly Rod	Conventional
❏	Bluegill	62	❏	❏
❏	Green Sunfish	63	❏	❏
❏	Longear Sunfish	64	❏	❏
❏	Redbreast Sunfish	65	❏	❏
❏	Redear Sunfish	66	❏	❏
❏	Redspotted Sunfish	67	❏	❏
❏	Warmouth	68	❏	❏

Black Bass

		Page	Fly Rod	Conventional
❏	Largemouth Bass	70	❏	❏
❏	Spotted Bass	72	❏	❏

Temperate Bass

		Page	Fly Rod	Conventional
❏	White Bass	23	❏	❏

Crappie

		Fly Rod	Conventional
❏	White Crappie	❏	❏
❏	Black Crappie	❏	❏

Miscellaneous Fish

		Fly Rod	Conventional
❏	Channel Catfish	❏	❏
❏	Spotted Gar	❏	❏
❏	__________	❏	❏
❏	__________	❏	❏
❏	__________	❏	❏
❏	__________	❏	❏

Additional Notes:

____

____

____

____

____

For further reading, and to support fishing in Sam Houston National Forest, visit
www.flyfishingthesam.com

4" x 2.6" sticker: The Trifecta of the Sam - Longear sunfish, spotted bass, and warmouth

3" x 3" sticker: Cottonmouth

A portion of the profits from the sale of items associated with *Fly Fishing the Sam* will be donated to various outdoor recreational causes. This includes, but is not limited to, the conservation of American wildlife and water resources, outdoor education, and further promotion of the American heritage of hunting, trapping, and fishing.